Beat Adversity and Aspire to Live (Empowerment)

by
Lorenzo Suter

Order this book online at www.trafford.com
or email orders@trafford.com

Most Trafford titles are also available at major online book retailers.

Printed in Victoria, BC, Canada.

ISBN: 978-1-4269-1512-3 (sc)
ISBN: 978-1-4269-1513-0 (hc)

Library of Congress Control Number: 2009934602

*Our mission is to efficiently provide the world's finest, most comprehensive book publishing
service, enabling every author to experience success. To find out how to publish your book, your
way, and have it available worldwide, visit us online at www.trafford.com*

Trafford rev. 11/02/09

 www.trafford.com

North America & international
toll-free: 1 888 232 4444 (USA & Canada)
phone: 250 383 6864 ♦ fax: 812 355 4082 ♦ email: info@trafford.com

Lorenzo's Ten Laws of Life

Take Charge Of Your Life on **Monday** And Be Responsible

Take Charge Of Your Life On **Tuesday** And Be Accountable

Take Charge Of Your Life On **Wednesday** And Have Determination

Take Charge Of Your Life On **Thursday** And Contribute

Take Charge Of Your Life On **Friday** With Resilience

Take Charge Of Your Life On **Saturday** With Perspective

Take Charge Of Your Life **On Sunday** With Faith

You say: "It's Impossible."

God says: All things are possible (Luke 18:27).

You say: "I'm tired."

God says: I will give you rest (Matthew 11:28-30).

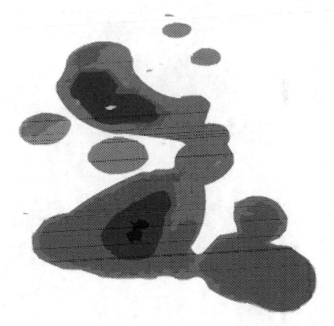

You say: "Nobody really loves me."

God says: I love you (John 3: 1 6 & John 2:34).

You say: "I can't go on."

God says: My grace is sufficient (II Corinthians 12:9 & Psalm 91:15).

You say: "I can't figure things out."

God says: I will direct your steps
(Proverbs 3: 5-6).

You say: "I can't do it."

God says: You can do all things
(Philippians 4:13).

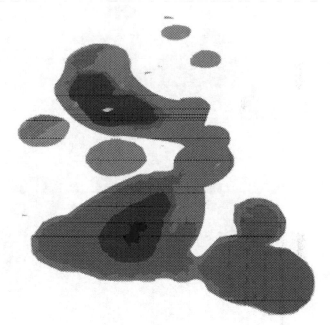

You say: "I am not able."

God says: I am able (II Corinthians 9:8).

You say: "It's not worth it."

God says: It will be worth it (Romans 8:28).

You say: "I can't forgive myself."

God says: I forgive you (I John 1:9 &
Romans 8:1).

You say: "I can't manage."

God says: I will supply all your needs
(Philippians 4:19).

You say: "I'm afraid."

God says: I have not given you a spirit of fear (II Timothy 1:7).

You say: "I'm always worried and frustrated."

God says: Cast all your cares on Me (I Peter 5:7).

You say: "I'm not smart enough."

God says: I give you wisdom (I Corinthians 1:30).

You say: "I feel all alone."

God says: I will never leave you or forsake you (Hebrews 13-5).

Introduction

Why does my life feel so empty? Why aren't all these things more satisfying? What's missing? Why am I so miserable? The answers we seek to fill our emptiness are difficult to find because we do not know where to look. We live in a material and outward society, so most of us naturally look outside ourselves for fulfillment – more money, more prestige, a better job, a different location, a new house, a higher degree, and so on. Most of us who have looked for answers for a while, through intellectual or physical activity, involvement, psychiatry, encounter groups, and even religion, realize that no one can give us the answers – we must find them for ourselves, within ourselves. And to find the answers, we can't care too much whether we find them or not. We must care only enough to keep searching.

Searching for Life

Life seems flat and stale to many people: they wonder why they do not grow or stretch, improve or learn. They believe they are stuck in a rut. They would like to get out of it. The answer to this problem is simple, although applying it is never easy. Men and women need detachment. Detachment means cutting all the strands that tie us to the ground. Gradually loosening the ties that bind us to external things will remedy a dangerous and unhappy state of attachment. Attachment narrows; detachment broadens us. One should seek happiness instead of lurking to find evil or sad thoughts.

Happiness

We all want happiness. If you are ever to have a good time, you cannot plan your life to include nothing but good times. We should all take this into consideration; it will make the attainment of happiness immeasurably easier. Pleasure is like beauty. Pleasure is deepened and enhanced when it has survived a moment of pain. Pleasure is a by-product, not a goal. Many people make the great mistake of aiming directly at pleasure; they forget that pleasure comes only from the fulfillment of a duty or obedience to a law.

Happiness can be attained under virtually any circumstances provided you believe that your life has meaning and purpose. The struggle that each individual goes through undermines their integrity. People are homeless because of their thought process. This process could have been created because of race, culture, economic status, friends, and family. Whatever the cause, our life is a challenge on a daily basis. Knowledge is strength that each individual needs in the world. Why isn't everyone rich? Why are some people poor? The chosen way of life has yet to be determined but the way of life and choices you make can be determined by mistakes, obstacles, and trials and tribulations. Mistakes and obstacles are splendid, breathtaking, tremendous, remarkable, astounding, humbling, and awe-inspiring. Mistakes are created to pour out knowledge. We should be able to learn from our mistakes and create a source of strength.

Simple and powerful awareness is the first step to take. If we force ourselves to have only one feeling about something, we experience mental anguish, stress, and discomfort. Once an emotion is created, it stays with us in the present moment until it is allowed to be expressed. We waste lots of energy and time trying to change feelings that exist within us. In addition to turmoil with an individual, the myth of singularity puts an unnecessary strain between people. When each person in a relationship is convinced that there is only one way to look at something, conflicts become very difficult to resolve.

When most people think of success they think of professional and material success. This type of success cannot be equated with happiness. There are, however, myriad forms of success that do lead to happiness: success in love, in relationships, in child rearing, in touching others' lives, in becoming deeper, in gaining wisdom, in doing good, and in learning about oneself.

Understood this way, fun is very important to happiness. Life has a great deal of stress and routine, and human beings need release from them. Fun provides a release. That is why we are much better able to deal with life's problems after a vacation. Fun can be injected into virtually every pursuit in life. That is where fun's great importance lies. If you can have fun while doing what is significant—raising a family, working at your profession, volunteering with the needy—you will truly be a happier person.

To be successful, you need to be motivated. To be motivated, you need to enjoy and care about what you're doing. If you hate, or even mildly dislike, your nine-to-five routine, you won't be able to give it your best, you won't learn as much as you could, you won't rise to the top, and you'll be exhausted by the time you return home at night.

You won't love your family, your friend, your neighbor because human love for other humans is not unconditional and many people have looked to God for unconditional love. This has profoundly helped many people live in an unloving world, especially if their earthly parents never gave them unconditional love. God's love of us is immense and forgiving (if we repent), but not unconditional. One must work at happiness and value different opinions to convey happiness.

Work

Work—very few people in this age do the kind of work they like to do. Instead of choosing their jobs from choice, they are forced by economic necessity to work at tasks that fail to satisfy them. But you don't have to live life doing something you don't like.

Normal people can achieve far beyond the norm due to an insatiable internal drive. Anyone who demands excellence in life despite few inherited advantages can achieve more. Many normal people with "abnormal" drives have achieved unbelievable success by living out their dream of reality. Simple people have used their vision, energy, passion, and tenacity to reach the top—these people dare to be different and thereby become rich and famous.

The life that we live should not be taken for granted. Every person should be involved, rather than doing nothing. The human drive is what makes the world go around and around. So many people live their lives expecting the "nothing" syndrome. "I care about nothing!" "I don't care about anything!" People should change the way they live their lives. The lack of knowledge causes poverty and unmotivated people. Many people do things because that's what their aunts, uncles, and friends did.

What, then, is the rightful limit to the sovereignty of the individual over himself? Where does the authority of society begin? How much of human life should be assigned to individuality, and how much to society?

Society

Society is not founded on a contract, and inventing one won't deduce social obligations or answer a good purpose. Everyone society protects owes a return for the benefit, and living in society means each person should observe a certain line of conduct towards the rest.

Decision requirements are those intuitions, judgments, and skills that must be mastered before a job can be reliable accomplished. Neither analysis nor intuition alone is sufficient for effective decision making. The synthesis between intuition and analysis that seems most effective puts intuition in the driver's seat so that it directs analysis of our circumstances.

Supposing this doctrine is one of selfish indifference would be a great misunderstanding. We can't pretend that human beings have no business in what others conduct in life and we should not concern ourselves about the well-doing or well-being of one another unless our own interest is involved.

Decisions

Our decisions depend on what people do and how they feel about that decision. People should make decisions on what they feel is right. Not what others think is right or wrong. **The lack of knowledge is one of the reasons why people do not reach success.** They fall between the cracks because they were told that they couldn't make it or because their mother, father, and family members didn't do anything in their life. This is considered, in my view, not using your mind. The practice of mindfulness is very similar on an emotional level in the way it affects our daily lives. It brings to the surface aspects of ourselves that are usually hidden in some way, or that we are frightened or ashamed of, embarrassed about, or simply unable to admit or deal with. Mindfulness is an enormously effective way to make peace with every aspect of yourself. Rather than being freaked out or stressed by your own worries, for example, you can learn to acknowledge your worried thoughts and feelings without being overly concerned about them. You begin to look at them instead of react to them.

Our Thought Process

Our thoughts randomly jump from planning to solving, or worrying to figuring to fantasizing and back again. Very few facts tell their own story, without comments to bring out their meaning. The whole strength and value, then, of human judgment, depending on the property, is that it can be set right when it is wrong. Reliance can be placed on human judgment only when the means of setting it right are kept constantly at hand.

Our thought process thrives on excitement and negative will power. People want to hear failure, problems, and adversity. You should trust in your abilities to do what you believe, your confidence gives you the will to make use of those skills. Not everyone is a basketball star, football star, or a famous, rich celebrity. Skills are equipped with integrity and an ambition to strive. Skills come naturally, but a person must use the skill at hand. Many people within our lifetime let their skills go to waste. We settle for nullity and we just do what everyone else is doing. This is so "common life" because we act in a mindset of common life people. Many people settle because everyone in their family settled. The skills go to waste because they do not have the willpower to expand. Many times in life it takes a strong energetic person to get another person moving in a positive direction.

When we are unhappy, we are faced with a great choice: do we recognize that life is inherently complex and filled with obstacles to happiness? Or do we blame others for our unhappiness? Of course, in some truly terrible instances—losing a loved one to a drunken driver, for example—blaming others for one's unhappiness is quite valid. But when most unhappy people blame others, they do so because that is easier than acknowledging life's complexity or searching within for the sources of their unhappiness.

Moreover, even when others do play a misery-inducing role in our lives, we still retain some control over our happiness. No matter how much outside forces may dominate our lives, there is one thing that we can virtually always control: how we react to them. We are responsible for making our own happiness. If you are used to being the master of your ship, it is empowering. But if not, it is frightening and therefore to be avoided.

Knowledge

Knowledge is endless and diffuse; philosophy is universal. Philosophers are interested in everything. But no man can know everything. Philosophy makes use of knowledge to reach the center. Mere knowledge is a heap, philosophy a whole. Knowledge is rational, accessible to every intellect in the same way. Philosophical thinking is a cast of mind that becomes part of a man's very nature. Interactions with other people are an important trigger of emotional responses. Also, since social situations are generally unpredictable, they are more likely to result in non-routine activities.

Knowledge can be a part of making the most of your time. But that means making choices, then working it out so you can do what you choose. Making the most of your time means doing nothing when nothing is what you want to do, and staying up all night to work on a project, read a book, or dance until dawn, when that's what you choose.

We can't always do exactly as we please for many reasons, including the need to earn a living, the desire to stay out of prison, and the hope of maintaining our key relationships. However, we can dramatically increase our life's options by decreasing our outside dependencies.

Personal Freedom

While numerous paths lead to personal freedom, our favorite is the path of most resistance—resistance to unnecessary expenditures of our three key assets: time, energy, and money. The more frugal you are with these assets, the less of them you commit to projects that have little meaning for you, the more you'll have for those that do, and the better you'll feel about the quality of your life.

Even if you take absolutely no intentional action to change your life, it will change. Time refuses to stand still. And as time moves on, we age with it, and our options change and often diminish. Therefore, the best time to begin fine-tuning your life is now and the best place to start is with something easy, where a small change can make a big difference in the quality of your existence.

The Choice We Have

Do we comprehend ourselves, then, through the freedom of our inner and outer actions? Once we understand our own judgments we confront them in greater freedom. But no understanding can comprehend the powers that produce the comprehensible meaning, which are nevertheless present in us. To recognize that we have a choice in all situations does not have a thing to do with whether or not we are in control of those situations. Remember the definition for wisdom: the growing lists of what we do not control and what we do not know. In the midst of these ever-increasing lists, we maintain authority over our lives, whether we like it or not, whether we admit it or not, and even whether we recognize it or not. We don't really have any choice in the matter. Resistance to change is natural. One must be mature in their thought process.

Maturity and Life

It takes maturity to avoid tempting but destructive choices; it takes maturity to want to be in control of your life and not to be controlled; and it takes maturity not to allow yourself in times of crisis to wallow in self-pity. The problem in our time is that maturity is not high on the list of goals we offer the next generation. We stress happiness, success, and intelligence, but not maturity. And that is too bad, both for society, which suffers when too many of its members are immature, and for the individual who wants to be happy. For happiness is not available to the immature. And one of the prominent characteristics of immaturity is seeing oneself primarily as a victim.

Become mature and read this book. Make great life choices! The overall objective of this book is to help you strengthen your intuitive decision-making skills and reach success. What defines success? The answer differs for each person. Is becoming a creative genius the same as success? Not for everyone. But for those willing to pay the price the road is accessible, and with effort they are able to tap into those key attributes necessary for creative genius.

Remember what you were taught about the right way to make important decision? You were probably told to analyze a problem thoroughly, list all your different options, evaluate those options based on a common set of criteria, figure out how important each criterion is, rate each option on each criterion, do the math, and compare the options against each other to see which best fits your needs. The decision is simply a matter of selecting the option with the highest score. This book aims to show that "nurture," not "nature," is the secret for becoming a creative genius.

Ingenuity: Law 1

The quality of being cleverly inventive or resourceful.

Ingenuity pertains to the law of life because in every circumstance, one must be inventive in different approaches. Life is monotonous if it has no goal or purpose. The first law of life, one must be clever to know where they are going. When we do not know why we are here or where we are going, then life is full of frustrations and unhappiness. When no goal or over-all purpose exists, people generally concentrate on motion.

When people use their ingenuity, they will think positive majority of the time and will not be depressed. A human being is very complex, made up of body and soul, flesh, and spirit, sensate in his love of pleasure, but rational in his thoughts and ideals. The use of ingenuity can allow one to do things that are not common to their lifestyle. It is important to note that ingenuity allows one to discover their self-image.

Our attitudes affect our aims, our aspirations, and our actions. Those who want to engage themselves creatively and constructively in Christian missions, must always be mindful of the motive, message, and manners of the Master. We cannot hope to help others to become Christians, if we, ourselves, do not reflect in our own lives the Spirit of Christ.

You will always have choices to make about what to do or not to do with the life entrusted to you by God. If we are faithful in our commitment to follow God's lead, we will lay our hearts open to Him by prayer. "God gives us light to go as far as we can see, but He does not light the path all the way to the end of journey."

Our English word "happy" comes from French and Middle English, and has to do with something that is accidental, something that happens by chance. But when we are blessed by God, we are self-contained; that is, our happiness does not come from circumstance, or by accidents, or though diligent searches. It comes because we stand approved before the Creator of the universe.   The bible tells us that God cursed the earth because of Adam's transgression. Sin and suffering cannot be separated. When sin came into the world, death and misery came with it. Those who understand the message of Holy Scripture eagerly await a new heaven and a new earth "wherein dwells righteousness." In that coming Kingdom there will be no more pain, suffering, disease, or death.

For an instant in time, you were "no-where"—the moment before your conception. Then in one holy instant, you went from "no-where" to "now-here." The tragedy of so many people is precisely that, to a great extent, they live mechanically: their thinking is stale, they don't examine their motives, and they respond to events automatically. They rarely take a fresh look at anything and rarely have a new thought. They exist at a low or shallow level of awareness. One of the consequences is that they live lives drained of color, excitement, and passion.

We often think we need the help of professionals, psychiatrists, psychologists, counselors, or clergymen, and indeed some of us do. But many of us do not need to spend long hours and many dollars in a professional's office. We just need to examine our lives instead of looking at other people's lives. Instead of working toward an idea, people keep changing the ideal and calling it "progress." They do not know where they are going, but they are certainly "on their way."

The benefit of ingenuity is to allow yourself to "think outside of the box" and defy the norm. One should be creative in their approaches. If you want to become a successful person, you must strive for excellence. You must not get defeated. The choices that allow you to do so are the strength and determination that you can do all things through the Supreme Being. Benefits of ingenuity entail cleverness, intellect, knowledge, ambition, and an understanding of behavior.

Comportment: Law II

Personal bearing or conduct; demeanor; behavior.

Comportment applies to the ten laws of life because one must have positive behavior in a successful life style. The benefit of comportment is when you can make a positive decision in a bad situation. When a person decides, as a basic pattern of behavior, to disregard external reality when it suits him or her and surrenders to the control of feelings, the chief feeling left to experience is anxiety. If we choose to move through life blindly, we have good reason to be afraid. Our behavior can dictate our desire to be secure and safe.

The desire to be rich often represents a deeply felt need for security and safety. Many people who are obsessed with making money fear that disaster is right around the corner. They perceive the world as an unsafe place where misfortune can fall upon them at any moment. Somewhere along the way, they formed the idea that money will protect them from destruction, or at least buy them out of it. This kind of fear is carried straight out of childhood. For a child to develop into a strong and confident adult, he needs parents who provide a certain amount of predictability, safety, tranquility, and orderliness.

This person really wants attention, recognition, acceptance, appreciation, admiration, and prestige. For the power-hungry adult, disappointment sets in when he discovers that exercising power over others does not really compensate for the vulnerability he experienced growing up. What he really craves is not to be impregnable or to possess superhuman strength, but simply to feel that his life is not running away with him; what he has the least control over are his own emotions, impulses, and behavior.

Gaining Insight

Managing ourselves and our actions is critical. Gaining insight is not enough; we have to apply this information to act more appropriately. Often, self-management is the most difficult thing we have to do. One of my peers recently pointed out that a study of successful and unsuccessful people found that the main difference was that the successful people could make themselves do the things they really didn't want to do. In many ways, this is the essence of self-management and a key characteristic of successful people.

Self-management really is management in every sense of the word, because it involves setting goals and establishing priorities. It involves using the information acquired from applying it in the stewardship of time, talents, money, etc. Self-managing is also about self-control, i.e., how well you control your words, emotions, and actions in relationships with others.

Because control is such a normal part of our lives, often it is overused. Over controlling does not work; it ignores human potential and disregards the boundaries of others. With a focus primarily on themselves and their agenda, controllers don't notice when they are trampling over someone else's legitimate personhood, territory, and related privileges. Typically, they justify their actions by the "good" work they do or the "crisis" we are facing. However, those on the receiving end do not feel empowered and more capable as a result. On the contrary, they feel less valued and then they take less ownership for their work.

This lack of wholeness or integrity causes major problems in every area of life. If you will take a moment to reflect on what you already know, you will see that most of our negative behaviors ultimately can be traced back to this one source of not feeling whole or sufficient. Consider the two extremes of low self-confidence and egotism. Both begin in feelings of inadequacy.

You would expect these feelings from those who say they have low self-confidence, but it's just as big a problem for those at the other extreme. In fact, its no secret among high achievers that their key motivators are often fear of failure, fear of rejection, fear of looking bad, fear of being financially poor, fear of disappointing people who believe in them, and fear of not achieving perfection. When people feel inadequate, they fear (even are ashamed of) being seen just like they really are.

It's not just high achievers though; most all of us try to prove ourselves successful to someone. These motivations can be used for good, but if the fear is strong enough and if a threat is big enough, or goals are blocked, negative behaviors easily show up.

Think back over some of the worst leaders and teammates you've had and recall the behaviors that put them in this category. You'll probably come up with a list that includes terms like dishonest, bullying, cowardly, jealous, manipulative, with-holding information, deceiving, not trusting of others, unwilling to delegate, controlling, passive, unappreciative, overly cautious, indecisive, gossiping, critical of others, selfish, envious, and procrastinating.

For some, these behaviors are aimed at building up self (power, money, control, reputation, etc.) to gain a feeling of being adequate, secure, sufficient, or superior. For others, it's an attempt to hide conscious feelings that they are weak and don't have it all together.

Even those who are the most secure display some of these behaviors, as well as others, but they are less severe and more acceptable. Think about the underlying drive in so many of our efforts to look good, whether through clothes, trim figures, athleticism, intelligence, our cars, or our homes.

Self-Oriented Behaviors

The issue we want to keep focused on is that these self-oriented behaviors can disrupt leadership, team unity, and performance. So the question becomes, "What can we do about it?"

When we are blind to something we tend to reflect what we are blind to in ourselves. A person who ignores a need tends to be blind to opportunities to satisfy that need. For instance, when a person denies his need and desire for companionship, he suffers from loneliness and does not see opportunities for friendship. A person who denies the reality of her pain tends to be oblivious to the source of the pain and continually exposes herself to new hurt. A person who guiltily disowns certain desires may, via the mechanism of projection, attribute them to others, as when we refuse to recognize our feelings of envy when we falsely attribute them to others.

We are not born with an ego or a sense of self. Both emerge and evolve over time. Essential to this process is the discovery of boundaries, learning where we end and the world begins. Among other aspects of growth, this unfolds our emotional life.

Once an emotion arises, it follows its own natural course: it is experienced, it is expressed in some form of bodily behavior, and it is discharged, to be replaced by some other emotion. This is the normal progression. When the process is blocked by denial or repression, unresolved tensions remain in the body—the emotion is dammed up, as it were—even if conscious awareness of the emotion has been extinguished or was never permitted to occur.

Of course, not every emotion need be acted on. An emotion carries within it the impulse to perform some particular action, but emotion and action are different categories, and such impulses need to be obeyed blindly and uncritically.

People can be inspired, stimulated, or coached to live more consciously, practice greater self-acceptance, operate more self-responsible, function more self-assertively, live more purposefully, and bring a higher level of personal integrity into their lives, but the task of generating and sustaining these practices falls on each of us alone.

Kindness, compassion, and selflessness don't lift people out of poverty. Liberated human ability combined with perseverance, courage, and the desire to achieve something worthwhile and (sometimes) make money in the process is what does it. But of course, such motives are not unselfish. And this is why people can accomplish "miracles."

You will experience another holy instant when you will go from now here to no-where. We call that moment death. Yet you—the divine, changeless, eternal, invisible—will live on. We control our destiny or it controls us. Visionaries have paved the way and many people still lack motivation, achievement, and thoughts. Instead many people have envy, hatred, no education, and they are looking tragedy in the face, which instills them with resilience and builds strong self-confidence and coping skills.

The benefit of understanding comportment is realizing your behavior. We often give feedback to others about their lifestyle and financial barriers, but we do not take time out to understand our behavior. Are you reading books for knowledge? Do you have goals? These are some questions that will allow you to understand your behavior. If you do not have any goals, then more than likely, your behavior is going to be streamlined to negative happenings. In other words, you are more susceptible to negative outcomes. The goal of comportment is to understand you and only you! Once you master this, you will gain acceptance to your goals, ambition, and career path. You will fully trust your thought process that you can accomplish anything you set your mind to.

Fruition: Law III

Attainment of anything desired; realization; accomplishment.

Fruition applies to the law of life because it emphasizes accomplishment. How would you like to live without pain? You would never have a headache. Your arthritis would disappear completely. How would you like to live without problems? You would have a perfect marriage in which you and your wife lived in harmony. Your children would obey your every wish and excel in their studies. Of course, I cannot tell you how to live without pain, problems, or pressure; however, I can tell you how to live *with* pain, problems, and pressure.

You can live victoriously with pain, pressure, and problems by perceiving daily that God loves you. This act is not based simply upon feelings. It is an act of faith based upon the Word of God. We can live victoriously with pain, problems, and pressure if we pray daily from a thankful heart. The apostle Paul had more than his share of pain, problems, and pressure. In almost every major city where Paul preached, he met fierce opposition. He was jailed, stoned, beaten, and cursed. If we are to pray daily from a thankful heart, we must focus on the positive and not the negative. If you expect the best, you will probably get it. On the other hand, if you expect the worst, you will probably get that. You can live victoriously with pain, problems, and pressures if you make it a habit to perform acts of love for others.

One must understand that they can accomplish their goals throughout life without any obstacle. The economy may be crashing, gas may be up, but you must stay steadfast and strive to overcome these barriers. Your thought process must entail that regardless of the happening, "I ____(Your Name)___ can do it. I can achieve it. I will do it. I will become a CEO. I will own my own company." The benefit of this law is to understand that you can but you must be self-driven to say, "No one can stop me except me." Content people stop themselves and one must understand that people do not stop people, you stop yourself.

Contentment: Law IV

The state of being contented; satisfaction; ease of mind.

Contentment is a law of life because one must understand that if you are content with your accomplishment, you may be content with your livelihood. Contentment is acquired through great resolution and diligence in conquering unruly desire. The principle cause of discontent is egotism, or selfishness, which sets the self up as a primary plant around which everyone must revolve. The second cause of discontent is envy, which makes us regard the possessions and the talents of others as if they were stolen from us. The third cause is the ordinate desire to have more to compensate for the emptiness of our heart.

To be content, we need to recognize out limits. Whatever is within our limits is likely to be quiet. For example, if you work a low paying job, you must understand your limit by not going to a car lot and buying Mercedes Benz that you cannot afford. Contentment, therefore, comes in part from faith in the purpose of life and being assured that whatever the trials are, they come from the hand of a Loving Father.

The chief cause of inner unhappiness is egotism or selfishness. He who gives himself importance by boasting is actually showing the credentials of his own worthlessness. Pride is an attempt to create an impression that we are what we actually are not. We should measure ourselves to see if we are content.

We measure the value of time by how we spend it. "How was your weekend?" a friend asks. "Wonderful," you respond, "I had a great time." Or, "Terrible," you reply, "It was a complete waste of time." If you spent a day doing something you enjoyed or that produced a desired result, you probably felt the day was good. On the other hand, if you spent the majority of a day doing something you didn't enjoy or that didn't produce a desired result, you probably felt the day was bad. Rich is not about money; rich is about life. And life is made up of one thing: time.

Most days, time takes more life from us than we take from it. And it's obviously not because we enjoy being stressed and frustrated and full of regret; it's because time is consistently more consistent than we are. Time is predetermined, set in perpetual motion by God "in the beginning," and you can't slow its pace or alter its consistency. That's why managing time is a bit unrealistic.

The notion of time management is not just a play on words, either. It represents a flawed understanding of time that affects how we react to our time frustrations. These busy days require a new solution—one that accounts for the fact that we cannot manage the clock; we can only manage our thoughts and actions.

- Life will never settle down until I choose to settle it down.
- Working is not living.
- Time is life first, then money.
- More work usually means less life; less work, more productivity and efficiency, usually means more life.
- How I use my time deeply impacts my self-esteem, my identity, and my fulfillment.
- I cannot control time, but I can control how I use and respond to time.
- I have known fear of failure, fear of humiliation, fear of injury, and sometimes fear of death, either for myself or a loved one. Most of all, I have wrestled against the fear of not mattering, of being cast out because I was not worthy.

The main focus of these bullet points is to inform you that contentment is based on not understating your identity. How much happier people would be if instead of exalting their ego to infinity, they reduced it to zero? The benefit of understanding contentment is that one may be content, but in order to reach a goal, one must bypass contentment to inhibit action. They would then find the true infinite through the rarest of modern virtues: humility.

Humility: Law V

The quality or condition of being humble; modest opinion or estimate of one's own importance, rank, etc.

Humility is a law of life that will carry its ways to the grave. Humility is truth about yourself. The humble man concentrates on his own errors, and not upon those of others; he sees nothing in his neighbor but what is good and virtuous. He does not carry his own faults on his back, but in front of him. The neighbor's defects he carries in a sack on his back, so he will not see them. The proud man, on the contrary, complains against everybody and believes that he has been wronged or else not treated as he deserves.

When the humble man is treated badly he does not complain, for he knows that he is treated better than he deserves. Perfection is being, not doing; it is not to affect an act but to achieve character. Nothing makes life unhappier than its meaninglessness, and life is devoid of meaning only when it is without purpose.

The challenging part about creating purpose is completing what's been left undone. Learn to surround yourself with the things that really please you and work for you, and edit out the things that don't; you'll see where your life is not working at maximum potential and you'll see places where you feel stuck, sluggish, perhaps confused. Lack of clarity or focus usually signals that something is incomplete.

The secret to a life of ease is cleaning up our messes and then designing a personal practice or system that doesn't allow them to recur. This is not difficult, and we can take it a step at a time. Let's look at the process of finding where you need to clean up. We'll identify exactly what needs to happen for you to get complete. You'll create your completion list and, as quickly as you can, get it handled. I promise you this: once you do your completions, you'll feel so good and so free that this process will change the way you deal with life.

Let's take a look at in-completions: things in your life that are unresolved and left hanging. Do you have big in-completions in your life? They can be notorious and contagious. One incompletion leads to another and so on. Focusing on creating and dreaming is difficult when you have bills that are overdue or clutter all over your home.

We don't need to obsess about order. We just want to recognize signs of disorder. When you have clothes or shoes strewn all around the house, dishes piled in the sink, or a desk buried under paper, you may feel out of sorts. When life is overly cluttered, often so are we. Learn to see objectively what's in your mental and physical space. Recognize where you're sloppy and clean it up.

Humility allows one to be self-confident and not arrogant. Self-confidence is not arrogant overweening. It is simply an interior strength that experience has taught us is justified.

Perhaps the key attribute of people at the top is that they are decisive. But there's a kicker: generally speaking, the big-picture decisions are reached through a long process of consensus building different from the Lone Ranger image that most imagine.

The decision-making imperative is primarily expressed day to day with no papers are left on the desk or e-mails in the in-box because those decisions are made as-they-go in real time.

Focus is the accepted wisdom that the ultimate test of management smarts is the ability to multitask is not supported by my observation. Rather, inherent in the executive style is the ability to keep a laser focus—albeit for only minutes or even seconds at a time—on whatever is in front of them until the matter is completed.

Senior executives are characterized by an ability to always keep in mind a few dominant priorities around which they organize their day-to-day activities.

Executives have two types of priorities in their lexicon: the important tasks that preoccupy him or her every day, week, and year; but also, equally important, priority themes.

Failure to meet deadlines, honor commitments, monitor staff, return calls, and keep track of long-term projects is the most underrated cause of chaos and failure in business life. Strong words, but true.

This law is important to success and I challenge you to research humility. Research humility to understand that humble people are happy people! Humility is a source of communication and I want you to fully grasp the term by looking for ways to be more humble in your life. The impact it has on your life will amaze you.

Intercommunication: Law VI

To communicate mutually.

Communication is a vital part of our daily routines. Communication involves at least two people: the sender and the receiver. The average speaker talks at about 160 words per minute, but we can absorb information at three times that rate. However, according to one study, we listen with only 25 percent efficiency. This accounts for many of the misunderstandings that occur with people. How do we communicate a message? Only 7 percent of our message comes through the word we use, 38 percent comes through our tone of voice, and 55 percent comes through our body language. The individual must be aware of everyday happenings.

Each person in life must discover three essential aspects of their lives: their credo, their competencies, and their confidence. Your values, your personal credo, give you the right words to say. Your capabilities, your competencies, give you the skills to turn your words into actions.

This law is important because we must be able to communicate our feelings, ambitions to have a successful life. We must understand our senses. We must communicate on a daily basis and the most successful people are masters of communications.

Senses: Law VII

Any of faculties, as sight, hearing, smell, taste, or touch by which humans perceive stimuli originating from outside or inside the body.

Our five senses are the portals, or gateways, through which the brain contacts the outside world. We rely primarily on our senses of vision and hearing because they tell us a lot about our environment. Our other senses—smell, taste, and touch—are less frequently and obviously called upon. To understand this better, close your eyes and try walking through a room. Instantly, the world around you changes radically. Sounds, smells, and spatial memories of your physical surrounding leap into consciousness. With vision gone, your sense of touch suddenly becomes paramount. Navigating even a familiar environment is a real challenge, and your brain goes into high alert.

Most of what we learn and remember relies on the ability of the brain to form and retrieve associations. Associations are representations of events, people, and places that form when the brain decides to link different kinds of information, especially if the link is likely to be useful in the future.

Senses of People

Comparing ourselves with people we think are happier than we are is not confined to comparing ourselves with the rich and famous. People compare themselves with anyone they think is happier. It can be cousin, an acquaintance, or most often, someone we barely know. In fact, the less we know about the people with whom we compare ourselves, the more dramatic the difference in assumed happiness is.

In daily life, most of us put on a problem-free demeanor. "How are things?" we are asked. "Fine," or even, "Great," is our automatic response, as it usually ought to be. Few of us really want to hear the problems afflicting everyone to whom we say, "How are you?" People who honestly answer are considered a pest. But we pay a price for everyone's putting on a happy face—we start believing that life for everyone else is great.

Senses of Happiness

One of the most common obstacles to happiness is the equation of happiness with success. If you equate happiness with success, you will never achieve the amount of success necessary to make you happy. You can always achieve more success. Another way to demonstrate that success does not equal happiness is to talk to highly successful people and find out if they are happy. Many times, they are actually unhappier than when they started out. Because they continue to equate happiness with success yet have not achieved happiness, they devote even more time to pursuing even more success. Therefore they do not devote time to doing those things that really would make them happier.

A third reason success does not equal happiness lies in why we pursue it. If success is very important to you, you must discover why. There are, to be sure, healthy reasons for wanting to enjoy success. Wanting some of the material trappings of success is healthy, especially financial security for yourself and your family. Wanting recognition for your achievements is healthy. Valuing the work you do and wanting to be successful at it is healthy.

However, if you want success because you think your happiness depends on it, or if you think your happiness depends on having ever-increasing amounts of money and recognition, this is unhealthy and not at all conducive to happiness. It behooves you to find out why you are so driven. Only then will you be able to recognize why success alone will not make you happy and to free yourself from relentlessly pursuing it.

If you ask yourself, "Why do I want success?" you may learn some interesting things. For example, many highly successful people have pursued success because their parent(s) gave them love only when they were successful. They have therefore pursued success to make themselves lovable. This is the one reason, incidentally, why envying all successful people is foolish—many of them are driven by demons that no amount of success can assuage. Knowledge can attribute to success and we must use our senses to reach our self-determined goals.

Knowledge: Law VIII

Acquaintance with facts, truths, or principles,
as from study or investigation.

Putting it in current terms, knowledge furthers experience and enables us to overcome or avoid difficulties and manage our conduct economically and efficiently. Knowledge that controls experience is discipline. It does not remain a mere instrument of control, direction, or economy in conduct, but enriches the experience and gives us culture. While then recognizing the enrichment of experience, the culture effect, and not limiting knowledge to mere instrumentality and device for the control of action is necessary. The origin and immediate purpose of knowledge, as information, as apprehending more facts and comprehending more principles, is a practical one: the control of experience. By a gift of grace, in getting that additional control of experience, we also get the culture effect and the added value in experience itself.

The fundamental educational considerations that result from this point of view would be, of course, the school motivating children to learn—an intrinsic and not simply factitious motive. I mean that when you want a child to acquire knowledge, when facts or principles are desirable for him to learn, they should be presented to make him see, at least feel, the relevancy of the knowledge and the impact it will have on his own experience. On the other hand, knowledge and learning should be applied. There should always be, not merely the possibility, but the necessity for applying the knowledge gained back to the better actual control of experience itself. Knowledge should not remain inert; it should enter into the formation of character—instruction should not end in itself, but should educate.

The possibility of knowledge becoming more than the mere accumulation of facts and laws, of becoming actually operative in character and conduct, depends on the extent to which that information evolves out of some need in the child's own experience and the extent to which the knowledge is applied to that experience.

Secret of Living

The secret of living a life of excellence is merely a matter of thinking excellence. Really, it's a matter of programming our minds with information that will set us free—free to be all God meant us to be. Free to soar! It will take awhile, and it may be painful—but what a metamorphosis!

The essential question isn't difficult to state: How can I, a person who has mediocre thinking, change? The best place I know to begin this process of mental cleansing is memorizing the all-important Scripture. I realize it doesn't sound very sophisticated or intellectual, but God's Book is full of powerful ammunition! And dislodging negative and demoralizing thoughts requires aggressive action.

Commitment

Choosing one thing over all the rest throughout life is a difficult thing to do. This is especially true when the choices are so many and the possibilities are so close. I believe that the way we approach an obstacle is simply in our state of mind. Will the obstacle defeat us? Will we rise above it? Believing the outcome determines the outcome. My problem was that despite my high school achievements as a debater and my later success in college, I stopped believing in myself. Sure, I wasn't letting other people limit my success—I didn't need to. I was doing it all on my own! Commitment brings self-discipline that does not need extensive monitoring. People who are fully committed put in discretionary effort. They not only do what they've agreed to do, they discover better ways to accomplish the work. They take on the objectives as their own. The may even come up with more ambitious goals and strategies.

At the opposite end of the continuum from commitment is resistance. Resistance means that one is opposed to your request or plan and tries to avoid carrying it out. Such resistance may be obvious or subtle. The person may seek to have the request nullified by upper management or may delay acting in the hope that you are not serious about it. Perhaps most damaging is hidden resistance, where the person pretends to comply but tries to sabotage the effort. Understanding your power will help prevent you from sabotaging your own success and the success of others.

Knowledge of Your Power and Influence

Your ability to gain other people's support is based on two factors: your power and your influence. In essence, power paves the way, making it easier for you to influence others and to gain their commitment. People often associate power with position on the organizational chart. The closer you are to the top of the chart, the more power you have. While that may indeed be true in many cases, it's only one part of the picture.

Essentially two types of power exist: position power and personal power. Position power is your potential to influence others based on your position in the organization. While that kind of power may be related to your place in hierarchy, the notion of position power is changing.

1. Authority or legitimate power: Your right to make requests of others, within the scope of your job responsibilities and role in the organization. While a boss obviously has authority to make requests of the people who report to her, everyone has this type of power to some extent.

2. Reward power: Your control over tangible and intangible things other people want. While the ability to control tangible rewards like pay increases or bonuses is often related to your position in the hierarchy, people through the organization can provide intangible kinds of reward such as a help and support.

3. Power over negative consequences: Your control over punishments or the denial of expected rewards. The power to create negative consequences is most often thought of as a top-down dynamic.

4. Information power: Your access to information other people need and may not be able to get from other sources.

We should relish any opportunity to acquire knowledge. Reduced to its simplest definition, education is training for the mind and the body. Education is the great conversion process under which abstract knowledge becomes useful and productive activity. It needs to never stop. No matter how old we become, we can acquire knowledge and use it. We can gather wisdom and profit from it. We can grow and progress and improve and, in the process, strengthen the lives of those within our circle of influence. We can enrich our lives dramatically through the miracle of reading and exposure to the arts.

The learning process is endless. We must read, we must observe, we must assimilate, and we must ponder that to which we expose our minds. I believe in the evolution of the mind, the heart, and the soul of humanity. I believe in improvement. I believe in growth. Nothing is quite as invigorating as being able to evaluate and then solve a difficult problem, to grapple with something that seems almost unsolvable, and then find a resolution. Most of the problems we talk about have to do with telling the truth, loyalty, and fairness, and they often involve matters of money, work, relatives, and friends. They present conflicts of values and interests. We seldom start our discussions agreeing about the right thing to do, and we often end in disagreement. Somewhere along the line, though, each of us has gained a better insight into the nature of morality. The dialogue has served its purpose.

Every person thinks. The fundamental nature of our brains is to produce thoughts. Sometimes these thoughts occur randomly, with no apparent connection to the moment we're living in; sometimes spontaneously in response to the stimulation of our immediate surroundings; sometimes in a detached, reflective, stepwise form of an internal dialogue, registered in our acquired native language. The challenge we face is not producing thought, it is producing useful thought. These are thoughts capable of analyzing the formidable but fascinating complexity of the world to guide actions to yield the most appropriate or best result.

Keeping one's emotional, impulsive reactions under control is absolutely essential for good, clear thinking. Broad, wide-ranging knowledge is also important. As our intellectual framework for perceiving and assessing the world becomes more stunted and fragile, we rely more on ideology, received knowledge, conventional wisdom, and blind faith to make our way through life. The psychological effect of this is a tendency to build shells that protect our identities, which are based on things we've been told and beliefs these things have engendered about the world. We tend to shy away from discussion about unpleasant things.

Personal power comes from two principal sources: expertise and admiration or identification. Expertise is your credibility as a source of advice, based on your knowledge and experience. Admiration or identification comes from people's esteem for you and their belief that you have exceptional qualities. Knowledge is important but once you get knowledge, you must familiarize your self with greed.

Greed: Law IX

Excessive desire for wealth of possessions.

Greed is an inordinate desire for more; an excessive, unsatisfied hunger to posses. Greedy people are forever discontented and therefore insatiably craving, longing, wanting, striving for more, more, more. Perhaps nothing is more tragic to behold than a greedy person—a person who is never fully at rest, always in pursuit of something else, something more, something beyond. The bondage this creates serves as an anchor so huge and heavy no set of wings, no matter how massive, can lift its victim to soar. This is an important law because we can start to exhaust of behavior and produce inadequate work because of greed.

The first and most common face greed wears is the green mask of money, money, money! Greed is an excessive motivation to have more money—a face we see all around us. Most people I meet in the workplace want more money for what they do. Before challenging that, stop and think of those you work around. Most are woefully discontented with their salary. And by the way, you don't have to be rich to be greedy. I know more people who don't have enough money and are greedy than I know greedy people with more than they need. Most often, greed appears as a gnawing, ruthless hunger to get more, earn more, and even hoard more money.

Greed often wears the face of things, material possessions. Greed is an excessive determination to own more things. Again, think before you reject that thought. We never quite have enough furniture. Or the right furniture. Have you noticed? To say it straight, greed is raw, unchecked materialism.

Greed can wear the face of fame. Greed is also an excessive desire to become more famous, to make a name for oneself. Some are so determined to be stars, to be in lights, they'd stop at nothing to have people quote them or to be seen in celebrity circles. Thankfully, not all who are famous fall into greedy category. It's wonderful to meet people who are stars and don't know it.

Greed can wear the face of control. Such greed is an excessive need to gain more control, to gain mastery over something or someone, to always be in charge, to call all the shots, to become the top dog, the king of the hill. The great goal in many people's lives is to manipulate their way to the top of whichever success ladder they choose to climb.

At risk of sounding terribly simplistic in my analysis, greed can be traced in Scripture to that day our original parents, Adam and Eve, fell in the garden. Where they turned their attention from the living God back to themselves, greed entered and polluted the human bloodstream. It has contaminated human nature ever since. In order for our greed to be controlled, a fight is inevitable. It is a battle for you, and it is a battle for me—a bloodless yet relentless warfare.

The first step in the battle is to discover the direction your old, often subconscious goals are pulling you, and then determine what's wrong with the direction. The second task is to identify and vocalize your thoughts for creating a new, consciously planned life.

The third objective is to take ownership and control over defining and then implementing your own new directions. Declare a new life direction! Everything we do as human beings can be viewed within the following seven all-encompassing areas.

1. Health: Our health is a dominate factor in our lives. It's been said in many ways that without your health, all the riches in the world are worth nothing. Health is more than the absence of disease or infirmity; it includes physical, emotional, social, and psychological well-being. Even a vague sense of ongoing dissatisfaction is not fully healthy. Successful people are aware that health is related to our physical, emotional, and mental abilities, each of which impinges on our success. Our bodies may be in top shape, but if our minds and souls are hesitant, we will lose in highly competitive athletic, business, or life situations.

2. Family: The family is the nucleus of our understanding about the world and our place in it. We grow up within the family and are driven to perpetuate ourselves through our own offspring. Family can be the ultimate support group that gives us the required emotional energy to tackle our life challenges. Lack of a supportive family has a strong influence on our goals and ultimate life direction. This basic building block of society shapes many of the early goals that become embedded in our psyche and influence our behavior through our early years. We derive much of our life understanding and involvements in the seven life areas through the family.

3. Spirituality: Our core beliefs about our purpose, the meaning of life, and the way to interact with others are formed through spirituality. These inner beliefs guide our attitudes, which in turn direct our life choices about goals to pursue. If our spiritual beliefs adhere to a strong, established system (such as a religion) for making choices in life, then much of our life becomes preordained: we follow the dictates of our belief system. If our spiritual beliefs are not strongly tied to an existing religious system, then we will invent some other set of core beliefs to help guide our choices through life.

4. Career: Your career is more than a job. It is your occupation, your way of earning a living, and the way you contribute to society. The jobs you obtain throughout life may change, but how you contribute to society usually shows a common thread throughout all the jobs. This common thread is your career. Your jobs might include being an at-home parent, or they might be in the trades or professional services. The personal satisfaction you receive from each of the jobs within your career is for you to measure. Remuneration for your career is one way of measuring success, but in itself, money may not be a fully satisfying measurement of success over the term of your life.

5. Recreation: People have pursued sports and hobbies throughout history. They give a balance, or a restful pause, to the other serious areas of our lives. Engaging in recreational pursuits enhances and strengthens other life areas.

6. Intimacy: Intimacy with another or a few others is the sticky glue that bonds people together. Intimacy helps to maintain stability in society and contributes to our self-confidence and self-esteem. People with low self-confidence don't perform at high levels. Those with low self-esteem don't feel worthy of making strong social contributions. Through intimate and familiar relationships with a few others, we increase our sense of self-esteem, allowing us to move forward and achieve goals, which reinforces our self-confidence and creates an upward spiral of success.

7. Community: The community is where we find our friends and associates—the individuals we consider our network. Our friendship networks help to formulate and modify our inner beliefs. Our friends also introduce us to other recreational and career pursuits.

The benefit of understanding greed is to understand your purpose with the health, family, spirituality, career, recreation, intimacy, and community. These are important because they allow one to develop their core principles, values, and beliefs. If you do not understand greed, you will allow yourself to be irresponsible.

Irresponsibility creates a careless attitude. When you get an abundance of things freely unloaded, carelessness emerges in an inability to discern the right scale of values. "What does it matter?" or, "Who really cares what I do with it?" That's the reason for the warning: "Watch yourself, lest you forget the Lord."

I took my fears and frustration and turned them into motivation. I wanted that dream of owning my own business, and no one was going to stop me, even if it did sound crazy. I have learned that you can create your own luck through opportunities that come your way. If you have a true passion and commitment to making something work and continually seek more opportunities to make that happen, anything is possible. When the next big opportunity comes knocking, clanging, and banging at your door, are you going to jump up and open the door or just ignore it? You will never know if it is the right opportunity unless you take a chance.

Success, I've found, fits no definable portrait or any preconceived model we might compare it to. Successful people are made up just like the rest of us—nothing different at all, other than success.

I've met many successful people in my life—people at the top of their game. People in every imaginable endeavor: business, the arts, medicine, science, politics, education. People from every country in the world. People of every age, from their twenties to their eighties. Married people, single people, gay people, heterosexual people, men, women, divorced people, committed-to-marriage people. People of every race, every ethnicity, every political leaning, from the most lividly left to the most righteously right. All were successful in their own way. There's no limit to the games these people have played or envisioned playing.

The essential question isn't difficult to state: How can I, a person who has absorbed so many years of mediocre thinking, change? For old defeating thoughts to be invaded, conquered, and replaced by new, victorious ones, a process of reconstruction must transpire. The best place I know to begin this process of mental cleansing is with the all-important discipline of studying scripture. One must defeat negative thoughts by combating mediocrity and irresponsibility thought processes.

Mediocrity

Combating mediocrity requires fighting fiercely in our day and time. Fast foods and quick fixes are the way of America and we expect change overnight. Fiercely changing with power must bond with an inspiration. The word "inspire" is a combination of the words "in" and "spirit." Inspiration involves a mind that transcends all limitations, thoughts, and bonds, and a consciousness that expands in every direction. By having courage to declare yourself as already being where you want to be, you force yourself to act in a new exciting and spiritual fashion. If you're living a life of scarcity, and all of the nice things that many people have are not coming your way, perhaps it's time to change your thinking and act as if what you enjoy having is already here.

Instead of continuing to tell yourself you are little more than a helpless victim, take charge. As soon as you catch yourself responding negatively or defensively, think: analyze the situation. To live above mediocrity, this level requires thinking clearly, thinking beyond today. Frankly, it requires dealing with selfishness and axing the roots of greed. Having come to terms with the importance of thinking clearly, we are ready to tackle the second challenge: living differently. Whoever clears away the mental fog is no longer satisfied drifting along with the masses. Vision replaces mental resistance. Determination marches in, overstepping laziness and indifference. And it's then that we begin to realize the value of priorities, a step that dictates the need for personal accountability.

We live in a negative, hostile world. Face it, my friend, the system that surrounds us focuses on the negatives: what is wrong and ugly, not what is beautiful; what is destructive, not what is constructive; what cannot be done, not what can be done; what hurts, not what helps; what we lack, not what we have. You question that? Pick up your local newspaper and read it through. See if the majority of the news doesn't concern itself with the negatives. It's contagious!

The following are three indisputable facts about the world system.

1. This negative mindset leads to incredible feelings of anxiety. Surround most people with enough negatives and I can guarantee the result: fear, resentment, and anger. Negative information plus hostile thinking equals anxiety. And yet Jesus said again and again, "Don't be anxious." The world system,

I repeat, works directly against the life God planned for His people.

2.   We are engulfed in mediocrity and cynicism (a direct result of living in a negative world). Without the motivation of divinely empowered insight and enthusiasm, people tend toward the average, doing just enough to get by. Thus, the fallout from the system is mediocrity. The majority dictates the rules, and excitement is replaced with a shrug of the shoulders. Excellence is not only lost in the shuffle, whenever it rears its head, it is considered a threat.

3.   Most choose not to live differently. Those who take their cues from the system blend into the drab backdrop of the majority. Words like, "Just go with the flow," and, "Don't make waves," and, "Who cares?" gain an audience.

By determination, I think of inner fortitude, strength of character, as disciplined to remain consistent, strong, and diligent, regardless of the odds or the demands. Priorities have to do with choosing first things first, doing essential things in the order of importance, bypassing the incidentals. And accountability relates to answering the hard questions, being closely in touch with a few individuals, rather than living like an isolated Lone Ranger.

By and large they sound good, and they seem to make sense out of the often confusing world around us. Even on college campuses, where one might expect a more serious and intelligent level of discussion, clichés seem to be our primary means of speaking to one another. While clichés have little depth of meaning, they do have power. Emotions are highly intense, fleeting, and sometimes disruptive to work; moods tend to be less intense, longer-lasting feelings that typically don't interfere with the job at hand.

Feelings

When people feel good, they work at their best. Feeling good lubricates mental efficiency, making people better at understanding information and using decision rules in complex judgments, as well as more flexible in their thinking. Too often at work, we try to stifle our feelings; yet even in a business environment, our emotional needs can be harnessed for positive communication and positive results.

To understand and deal with the dynamic nature of emotions in the workplace, the following eight principles are important to keep in mind:

1. Emotional needs always express themselves one way or another.

2. Anger is an expression of need.

3. Our feelings and needs are not wrong or bad.

4. Emotions are the gateway to vitality and feeling alive.

5. We can address our emotions and still save face.

6. Immediate reactions to problems often disguise deeper feelings.

7. We must clarify individual needs before problem solving with others.

8. We need to communicate both positive and negative feelings.

These practices of understanding greed can impact feelings, emotions, and overall objective of life. Reflect on mediocrity and streamline your responsibilities to a positive outcome. These practices can benefit your life because they allow one to cultivate their on way of life.

Christianity: Law X

Belief or Practice.

Our world is characterized by startling and significant changes. These are constantly, consistently, and continuously confronting and challenging Christianity and the cause of Christ. The great danger of our times lies in the fact that we tend toward secularization, automation, commercialization, dissipation, dislocation, disintegration, and degradation. We all have the same problem: all have sinned and come short of the glory of God. Christians do not assume that others have a problem; we assume that we have a problem. There is no basis for pride in the doctrine of sin; we have all missed the mark.

This awareness does two things: it provides us with healthy skepticism and healthy humility. In the first place, our universal problem should make us leery of any arguments that focus entirely on one particular problem. We ought not to be surprised by sin; and we ought not to assume that any single solution will entirely resolve the problem. That doesn't mean we stop trying, of course; the fact that your children are sinners doesn't mean you stop training them. Training makes a difference.

Our underlying assumption about sin should also give us a healthy humility. One thing I have understood is the existence of arrogant Christians. I find that a contradiction in terms. How can we, who understand our own poverty before God and his grace in our life, have even a stitch of arrogance? Recognizing your own sin doesn't make you feel superior, it makes you weep and seek mercy. And when you receive forgiveness you are overjoyed and deeply humbled. The one thing you can't possibly feel is superior or arrogant.

Recognizing our sin, then, doesn't separate us from others; it joins us to one another—in our common predicament and our need for the grace of Christ. Jesus Christ is the Truth, and the Truth calls us to love others as ourselves. What is true, and what does the truth require of us?

John puts it like this: "In the beginning was the Word, and the Word was with God, and the Word was God. . . . The Word became flesh and made his dwelling among us" (JN 1:1, 14). Jesus Christ is the embodiment of truth, because he is the incarnation of God in human form. Those who wish to know what it means to live in truth will need to pay attention to him.

And what does the truth require? That we love God and love others as ourselves. Christians are to be known for their love. It is our mark of authenticity. "Let us not love with words or tongue but with actions and in truth. This then is how we know we belong to the truth" (1 Jn 3:18-19).

It seems to me that this connection between truth and love is especially vital as we confront the issue of our differences. But what does this love entail? First, it calls us to love God. And that means, among others, listening to his Word. Enjoying his creation. Obeying his commands. Acting according to his will. Setting our hearts in tune with his. Honoring him with our gifts. Doing what is right. Forgiving others as he has forgiven us. Being good stewards of his world. Loving justice. Doing mercy. Walking humility.

Conclusion

And so it turns out that the people of truth are not those who are good with words, but those who are good with actions. Those who only defend the truth with words and don't act in love are a noisy gong, a clanging cymbal.

Do take time to think about the goals you want to pursue and do consider goal possibilities in all aspects of your business or life. This provides a balanced approach. It improves your chances of maintaining momentum and staying on track.

Don't fail to write your goals down, and don't rely on your memory to provide the mental focus and conscious and subconscious reminders necessary for pursuing your goals.

Don't view goal setting as an activity you do just once a year. Goals are tools for growth, and your goals should be continually growing and changing. An important aspect of setting goals is to drive your vision and plans for achieving them into your subconscious mind so you are on autopilot.

Do look at goal setting as an evolving process you will continue on a lifelong basis with ever-increasing and changing goals. Don't select goals without specifying a deadline and a timeline for completion. Our minds operate at the subconscious level with an undeniable and extremely reliable built-in clock and sense for time parameters. We generally put off things when no impending timetable or deadline exists.

Don't select generalized, non-specific goals. Our minds are bimolecular information-processing miracles, but they cannot and will not process generalized information. Generalized goals such as "improve quality" or "get rich" are meaningless until you define the terms "quality" and "rich."

Don't select just end-result goals. End-result goals are important, but they are not all that is required because end results are not doable, per se. You can't do a goal like "save money for a college education."

You can establish a savings plan that will accumulate into the amount desired. The actions are cause goals or action-supporting steps, and these are what you do.

Don't share your goals or your plans for pursuing them with more people than necessary. Some people, family members, and friends included, don't really want you to pursue and achieve your goals. This is not because they do not love you or think well of you, but because they are comfortable with you as you are. When people become aware that you are pursuing goals that may separate you from them or change how they know you, they may unconsciously resist your efforts.

Do create a variety of visible reminders of what your goals and plans for pursuing them are. There is no one way to do this. Using a variety of physical reminders is better than selecting just one that can become so obvious you ignore it.

Don't pick small goals that are easy to achieve. The biggest reason to have goals is to use them as tools for stimulating and guiding your business and personal growth and development. This means you must exert effort to stretch from where you are to where you want to be.

Small goals produce small power. Do pick big goals beyond your comfort zone so you can grow to new levels. Big goals force you to develop your skills and get better at doing what you have to achieve them. Big goals are inspiring. They provide pulling power and a targeted magnetic focus for you energies.

If it were a perfect world, we would have received everything we needed to feel whole and secure. But since it's not, we all have some degree of insecurity. What we needed and did not get is called unconditional love; and for those who get squirrelly when they hear the word "love," call it "acceptance." Either way, no one has received enough. Therefore, no one is capable or whole enough to give it adequately to others.

Once we come face to face with our personal roadblocks, we have two choices. We can say, "That's just me; that's just the way I am and I'm not changing." Or we can take the path to growth. All too often we choose the former, because the latter requires brutal honesty about ourselves and the challenges of change.

We resist change for many reasons, but the underlying provides a classic example of what one has to live with to continue to change and grow into the person he or she is called to be.

Generally, change has no quick-fix. Unfortunately, behavioral changes are usually not onetime events; rather they are a process. The process starts with knowledge or awareness. Then comes a plan. Then we take action, get feedback, analyze and critique, gain new insights, refine the plan, and then execute again.

The reward of positive change is growth, and that means you will become better equipped to deal with every aspect of life. Performance improves, you are more effective, you are a better teammate, and all your relationships improve. You can also expect less stress, which means better health and a more enjoyable life.

The kind of personal growth we've been talking about also means that you could unload some baggage and maybe even receive more unconditional acceptance. And think of the increased self-confidence that can come from a closer alignment of who you want to be and who you really are. With all that going on, you could gain freedom from the shame and guilt hiding in the dark rooms.

If you want to give your family a reward, if you want to give them a blessing like nothing you've ever done before, then walk this road of change and personal growth. The third law of planting says the harvest comes in multiples. Thus your changed behaviors will have a ripple effect that will keep going, even as a legacy to the third and fourth generations.

God laid out a principle with Abraham that I believe operates today in all our lives. By faith, Abraham left his home behind and moved to a new land. God honored his faith and actions and promised him, "I will bless you and you will be a blessing to all people." When we let go of and leave behind our old negative behaviors and baggage, we are blessed and others are blessed in the process. Now that's a reward that keeps on coming and enables us to keep on giving.

To be afraid is to suffer. Fear constitutes the most intense form of human oppression. When you are afraid, you cannot be happy. Fear is the single most destructive emotion in the heart's armory, the single biggest roadblock that you will encounter in your search for fulfillment and happiness. If you live with fear, you can be sure that you will die with most of your dreams unfilled. Unless you conquer fear, it will conquer you. Fear not only prevents you from fulfilling your greatest destiny, but it threatens to rob you of your identity by destroying everything about you that is unique. To be afraid is to be transformed from a human being of destiny to a creature with no future.

Fear is a permanent tormentor. Fear is an epidemic sweeping America and the world. We are more afraid now, with less cause, than we have ever been before, which largely explains why we are so unhappy, so easily shaken, so easily stirred.

We can fight back; declare that we are not at the mercy of our fears. It is time to fight back, to declare that we are not at the mercy of our fears. It is time to join the battle in a constant and daily struggle to conquer our apprehensions: to understand why they plague us and find a way to purge them from our lives so that we can finally be free.

In the modern world, tremendous forces bear down upon us: financial pressures, work pressures, political pressures, familial responsibilities, the fear of random and inexplicable violence, and the fear of illness, just to name a few. We are constantly confronted with the horrors of history and life: senseless hatred, poverty, famine, lovelessness, loneliness, and death. In a world of Godliness, bereft of soulfulness, we feel hollow on the inside and so succumb to outside pressures.

Despair means we have lost hope. As long as the future stands open and we can hope to draw some good out of evil we see or suffer, we need not despair. On analysis, then, it turns out that most despair arises because our focus has become too narrow. We have looked only at our own resources, found them woefully lacking, and so concluded that the future is hopeless. When we cast our net more broadly, availing ourselves of the resources of other people and the mysteriousness of life (the resources of God), our spirit may lighten. Other people may have good ideas about where we can gain some help. The mysteriousness of life may suggest that nothing is impossible with God, because God can make all things new. The mere possibility that this could be so is enough to drive away despair. To have realistic hopes, we need only to recognize the possibility that we can outwit the cancer, at least for a while, or that AA might help our sick spouse, because it has helped so many other alcoholics.

Pain puts the sharpest edge on our troubles. When we writhe in physical or emotional agony, we call life hateful. Indeed, we do well if we refrain from calling God hateful: who but a sadist would allow such suffering? Around the world millions of little children starve, millions more live worse than wild animals. Life is not pleasant; when we let ourselves see the enormities of human suffering. In ages past, as in our own time, the powerful grind down the weak. Disease and ignorance blight the lives of the majority. "Reality" is not pretty.

One must be tough to face pain. Yet facing pain is inevitable. Pain is horrible, a thing accursed. It is wrong to be sure it will defeat us. Sometimes physical pain is beyond our handling. We can only hope the morphine will be strong enough. Often emotional pain submits to loving attention. If others hold us, literally or symbolically, they can rock away our worst hurts.

Fear does not seem so formidable to me as pain, yet I don't doubt that it causes great suffering. People who live in the midst of violence, in terrible households, or neighborhoods dwell in an outpost of hell. People trapped in the midst of warfare—pawns in a brutal game—do well not to break from the strain.

So people around the world suffer from fear, a great cruelty. If we didn't grow up in a secure family, protected by love and a minimal prosperity, we began life with a solid strike against us. The wonder is that so many of us survive unpromising beginnings. We carry deep scars, but we keep struggling to move forward.

One of the worst aspects of fear is that it can numb our emotions and paralyze us. Afraid, we can stay in the crossfire, unable to move forward or back. Sometimes we eventually realize that moving would cost less than staying stuck, but often we overcome the paralysis of fear only if others pull us out.

Fear is a hardship, but not unusual. Indeed, often it makes great sense. The life swirling outside can be something we ought to fear. We have only two significant options when we experience genuine anxiety. We can accept the assurances of people with some claim to authority, some mantle of wisdom, and trust that existence will hold together enough for us to make our way through our years, be they many or few. Or we can experience directly, for ourselves, forces more powerful than death, dissolution, nothingness, even evil. We can learn in our own minds and hearts that love or life or being or, maybe, sheer determination, simple cussedness, can preserve us.

When we feel helpless, whether from anxiety or weakness or loneliness, we are stuck in our troubles. We can see no way out, so we curl up to await the worst. Still, we are never completely helpless. You have at least two distinct ways of letting go. One is negative, closing ourselves to any future possibility of change. The other is positive: "Things have passed out of my hands, but maybe my hands are not the only factors."

When we feel pain, fear, anxiety, helplessness, or any of the many other negative emotions, our sense of value and possibility shrinks. We believe we are not worth much and have little future. On the other hand, when we feel confidence, courage, and the other positive states of emotion, our being expands, many more things seem possible. The etymological roots of confidence suggest a faith and strength that bring us together. The roots of courage suggest a great heartening. What can we do to invite or reinforce these beneficial feelings?

You have been facing the wrong way! The most important insight you can have is to realize that you have been facing the wrong way for the better part of your life. The primary energy that you have used all your life is the outer energy. This outer energy is life sustaining but does not provide the sense of fulfillment and bliss that we long for. You have within yourself power to transcend the ego-dominated life. You can turn around and face inward, directly contacting your spiritual nature. You can then live each of your days, regardless of what you may be doing, with the sense of bliss that comes from being on the path of your sacred quest.

Religion is not primarily a set of beliefs, a collection of prayers, or a series of rituals. Religion is first and foremost a way of seeing. It can't change the facts about the world we live in, but it can change the way we see those facts, and that in itself can often make a real difference.

The starting point to your sacred quest is understanding that the universe and our participation in it are not haphazard things. What sort of world would it be if God didn't exist? Some people would say it would be a world very much like the one we now have, a world of war and threats of war, crime and corruption, and random cruelty. For me, the answer is even more dismaying. Without God, it would be a world where no one was inspired to put an end to them. I would be a world where, if we were the victims of crime or misfortune, we would curse our bad luck, and if someone near us was a victim, we would merely feel relief that it happened to her and not to us. But we would have no reason to feel this is not the way the world is supposed to work, nor would we have any reason to believe, with enough time and effort, we could make it better.

A world without God would be a world in which gravity pulled us down and there was no counterforce to lift us up, to cleanse us if we had sullied ourselves when we stumbled and fell, and assure us that we were worthy of a second chance.

And worst of all, in a world without God, we would be alone—no one to help us when we had to do something hard, no one to forgive us when we had disappointed ourselves, no one to replenish us when we had used ourselves up, and no one to promise us that, even when it was over, it will not be over.

Life Reasoning

Everything and everyone that came into your life had a reason for being there. They taught you lessons. Having a personal history keeps us from now. This is a radical idea perhaps, but I am asking you to consider the possibility of totally eradicating your personal history from your consciousness and simply living completely in the present moment.

The first thing that might pop into your mind, as it did into mine when I began to consider this possibility, is that it is impossible. I do have a memory, and it would be folly for me to pretend that I am not the product of my past. What I am asking you to develop is a "forgetery" to go with your memory.

The point is that as a product of your past, you dance to a tune thrown at you by others. In order to take the step up toward your sacred quest, you must toss out the idea that you are unable to take those steps in the first place.

Your personal history has attempted to convince you that you are one or several of the labels that you have been assigned. Ultimately, you adopted the labels as whom and what you were. In the process of erasing your personal history, you need to remove all the artificial labels.

You are not you name—your name was given to you to help distinguish your body from the other bodies around you, and to give others a word to use when they refer to you. But don't for a moment think that your name is who you are. Indeed, it is who you are not.

Dropping your personal history involves shedding the notion that you are what you do. Remember this exercise in logic: if you are what you do, then when you don't you aren't.

When you hold your personal identity in your work, you perform your routine in order to feel important. You work even though it no longer makes sense. You perform those tasks as if somehow the divine you were involved in this drama.

Why do good people do bad things? If we all have an innate need to think of ourselves as good, why do we do things that undercut our sense of our own goodness? Some people embrace a religious life out of a desire to live at the highest moral level, to exult in spending every waking moment conscious of the presence of God. But others commit themselves to a religious life because they are troubled when they find themselves doing things they know are wrong. They give in to temptation. They lie rather than tell the truth. They take shortcuts, gaining by cleverness and fraud what they want and cannot get by honesty.

Some people use religion to strengthen their immune systems and help them resist temptation. Some use it as an antibiotic to cleanse their systems of infection and make them feel healthy again. And some use it as an aspirin, to take away the pain of wrongdoing without affecting the cause of that pain.

Good people do good things, lots of them, because they are good people. They do bad things because they are human. In the daily, if not hourly, wrestling matches that set the tone of our lives, sometimes the angel wins and sometime the angel loses. With luck, we will not be overwhelmed by guilt when the egotistical impulse defeats the angel, and we will understand that the victory is temporary, not permanent, when the angel wins. We will understand that, to be human, we need them both. But we will never stop asking ourselves, "What kind of person do I want to be?" Why do people do things that should be easy to recognize as unacceptable? Are people naturally bad, and is good behavior only a thin veneer, the result of social pressure and the fear of being caught? No doubt some truly evil people live in the world, but probably fewer than we think.

The need to feel important drives people to place enormous value on such symbols as titles, corner offices, and first-class travel. It causes us to feel excessively pleased when someone important recognizes us, and to feel hurt when our doctor or pastor passes us on the street without saying hello, or when a neighbor calls us by our sister's or brother's name.

What to do? How can we find a place to stand that is free from the influence of money so as to think impartially about it and then plot our course according to deeper values?

People need to hear the message that they are good. And people who are not entirely sure of their goodness may need that validation even more. That may be why churches and synagogues attract people who are bothered by the lapses in their behavior as husbands and wives, as parents, and as children of aging parents, and crave the reassurance that they are welcome in God's house. They may be a wealthy businessman who cherishes a twenty-five dollar plaque given to him by his church, synagogue, or lodge for being honored as Man of the Year. It may explain why we do things that don't benefit him economically but psychologically: making charitable donations, volunteering for good causes.

How do most of us handle our mistakes? We blame others, we blame our upbringing, and we rationalize what we do to reassure ourselves of our essential goodness. We human beings are such complicate creatures. We have so many needs, so many emotional hungers, and they often come into conflict with each other. Our impulse to help needy people or support medical research conflicts with our desire to have the money to buy all the things we want. My commitment to doing the right thing impels me to apologize to people I have offended, but my desire to protect my image and nourish my sense of righteousness persuades me that the problem is their hypersensitivity, not my behavior.

What happens when our need to think of ourselves as good people collides with our desire to betray our values, violate our consciences, in our struggle to impact the world? Often we don't like what we find ourselves doing (although it is remarkable how easily we get used to it after the first few times), but we tell ourselves we have no choice. That is the kind of world we live in, and that is the price we have to pay for claiming our space in it.

Our souls are split, part of us reaching for goodness, part of us chasing fame and fortune and doing questionable things along the way, as we realize that those two paths may diverge sharply. Our self-image is like an out-of-focus photograph, two slightly blurred images instead of one clear one. Much of our lives, much of our energy will be devoted to closing that gap between the longings of our soul and the scolding of our conscience, between our too-often conflicting needs for the assurance we are good and the satisfaction of being told we are important.

Each of us is human, subject to the problems that afflict humans. We should not tolerate laziness, dishonesty, or betrayal. But neither should we condemn others for such apparent lapses. Instead, we can reach out to help them carry the burdens of sickness and financial difficulty, and even the weaknesses and shortcomings with which they grapple. None of us needs someone who only points out our areas of weakness and the ways we fall short. We need someone who encourages us to go forward, to try again, to reach a little higher this time. Excellence is difficult to achieve in a vacuum.

People want to know what it means to be moral and how to achieve this. They are troubled by the conflicts they sometimes experience between personal happiness and social responsibility; they often have difficulties weighing the options for action when no course seems right. We are uncertain about the relationship between practical outcomes and principled positions.

People are punished if they do something wrong, but not if they couldn't have done otherwise. We do not hold someone responsible if he has acted under duress. If a person steals money because someone else held a gun to his head, the person isn't a thief. Morality has meaning only for those with free will, that is, those who, when faced with a decision, are capable of freely choosing one thing or another.

People also aren't culpable if they can't understand the difference between right and wrong. The mentally incompetent aren't liable for their actions. And this is why, given what we know about the nature of other creatures, moral responsibility applies only to human beings.

When we start talking about why people do things and their mental capacity to understand, we leave the area of philosophy and move to psychology. Philosophy tells us that only those who have free will can be held liable for what they do. Psychology tells us that bells aren't liable for the damage they cause because bells can't reason and therefore have no free will. Responsibility requires some intelligence and/or mental competence. Therefore, a person may have committed a crime but can be found not guilty as result of insanity or mental deficiency.

Some things are part of our spiritual destiny and we just can't change them: certain instinctive attitudes and impulsive actions, the inability sometimes to act when we know we should, the way we sometimes allow ourselves to be drawn into situations against our better judgment, and, the biggest thing, our reactions to the urge to fight, to shout, to protect, to hide, to dictate, to shrink back, to control, to run.

Growing up means seeing the world as it is. Really growing up means realizing that the world really may be as you see it. Those who complain that they don't have the power to achieve their aims are forgetting this simple rule: holding a certain position will give power, but it is temporary unless you also have personal power. Personal power is defined as the strength that comes from making and maintaining sincere and deep interpersonal connections with others.

Life is a mix of the old and the new, the stable and the dynamic, the changing and the changeless. Change has always been a natural part of human growth, firmly established in the life cycle, which begins before birth and ends at death. Changing as a baby to become a person who not only gestures and gurgles but also crawls, walks, and talks, activating a wider use of the senses. Changing as a child to become a person who experiences a more complete sense of autonomy, identity, and unique worth. Changes in our lives brought about by positive growth add to our resources for living. We develop stronger bodies, minds, and spirits. We increase our knowledge and skill.

Not only do our personal situations change but so do our group experiences with others. We change in relation to and with other people. While the family is the primary group in which change occurs, the church, the school, and the work settings are examples of other groups in which change occurs in a variety of ways.

At work, changes happen in organization structures, such as adding or merging departments, forming new work groups or task forces. Change is not a new demand on the human race. Because change can have negative or positive consequences in our lives, we cannot afford for it to be loose. The changes in our lives need to be linked to a purpose that makes life worth living.

Every time we experience change, we go through processes that have some common elements. Some natural forces work in us. Some natural dynamics happen. Life is patterned in predictable ways. These patterns help us deal with demands. Much of this patterning has the labels of the above list—beliefs, attitudes, values, habits, relationships, roles, structures, norms, rules, and schedules.

To be a master of your universe you must understand your objective, the tangible end that, when attained, will leave you proud, and satisfied. You must understand how to create a viable plan to achieve your objective with an emphasis on acting as quickly as possible so that your experiences and learning will help you achieve your ends. One must also understand how people in your life and dynamics of your relationships with them contribute to your movement toward the objective.

Accepting yourself includes accepting the circumstances that come your way. Part of acceptance is viewing what is real and right without judgment, justifications, explanations, or blaming oneself or others. We are all affected by events outside our control; we can only control how we respond to them. Our ability to choose response depends entirely on our ability to see situations clearly and accept the reality. Then we can change things.

Change is important to your success. It takes a strong person to lead. Lead the change. Have you ever thought of how you changed your shoes, clothes, and your soap? We change every day of our lives. Some things are changed for the good and others for the bad. Do not change yourself to be like the people of this world, but change within by a new way of thinking. Then you can decide what God wants for you; you will know what is good and pleasing to Him and what is perfect. Many times people change clothes because of others. Have you bought a name brand shirt because you saw a celebrity wear it? Why? Do not change yourself to be like people of the world. Don't make this mistake because if you do, you will see your lift drifting away. So I tell you: live by following the Spirit. Then you will not do what your sinful self wants. Our sinful selves want what goes against the Spirit, and the Spirit wants what goes against our sinful selves. The two work against each other, so you cannot do just what you please.

Change is important—change your old ways for the positive. Paul said I want to give you some help; I want to tell you how to run the race of life. Run the race that is set before you. Run forward in the race of life toward a goal—set a goal and run toward it. That is foolish to tell a runner to run forward; does not everybody run forward? Oh no! Not in the race of life.

Many people run circles in the race of life. They have no aim, no purpose, no goal. If you are going to run the race of life, you should win it. You have to have a goal. In the game of life if you win the game, you win abundant life here and eternal life hereafter. You win what God wants you to have when he made you in his own image. If you lose the race, it literally means the loss of life, the loss of meaning, the loss of significance in life, and eternally, the loss of life itself, which is death.

I know others who run backward in the game of life. They are defeatists and pessimists. They are discouraged—life has gone by them and left them in the past. Life does not seem worth living if it has no goal or purpose. On the other hand, life is thrilling if it has a destiny.

What we call the ultimate purpose of life is one beyond all immediate or proximate goals, such as a man wanting to become a farmer, or a woman wanting to become a nurse. The purpose that survives when these lesser goals have been achieved is the ultimate goal. No one can have two final purposes in life any more than he can walk to the right and left at the same time. Knowing belongs to man's intellect or reason; loving belongs to his will. The object of the intellect is truth; the object of the will is goodness or love.

Fear is the emotion that rises in us when danger faces something or someone we love. The catalogue of fears is the catalogue of loves. Love is attraction for an object; fear is flight from it. Fear is a flight from a future evil that so exceeds our power that we cannot bear up under it. If we only knew it, we fear the wrong things. We used to fear God; now we fear our fellow man. The negative side of fear is dread, but the positive side is longing. Once such an individual turns to God, his fear turns to yearning and he discovers peace. The right kind of fear can be the pathway to peace. Two kinds of fear exist: the servile fear and the filial fear.

Servile fear is the fear of punishment, such as citizens have for a cruel dictator. Filial fear is the fear of hurting someone we love. Servile fear, or the fear of punishment, or dread, can be the starting point for filial fear. Dread can become longing. Without God, souls have misery but not mercy; they have the wounds, but not the physician. Misery is anxiety without God; mercy is anxiety with God.

Do you tolerate making bad decisions? Understand the following principles concerning tolerance: 1. Tolerance never refers to persons.

2. Tolerance always refers to evil, real or imaginary, never to good. Tolerance never refers to good. The good is never to be tolerated; rather it is to be approved, it is to be loved. You never say, "I'll tolerate a beefsteak dinner."

Life calls for thought and philosophy. What do we believe about life? If we believe in God, we must believe that life is not a fate but a privilege. The real problem is not life as we find it today. It is life itself. Life and the world have always been problems. We find ourselves alive on this physical earth.

We do not know the ultimate purpose of God; the most we can do here is to see and to know "in part." But we can see the out-working in time and space of a vast plan rooted in eternity. Our ultimate purpose is something far greater, more far-reaching, nobler, more generous than most of our forefathers could imagine.

Life is a mix of the old and the new, the changing and the changeless. The changes we experience are sometimes pluses—a new job role, Christian conversion. At other times the minus sign dominates—a tornado destroys a house, illness takes a life, a wife divorces her husband, a boss fires an employee. Change has always been a natural part of human growth, firmly established in the life cycle, which begins before birth and ends at death. One must be able to have (1) humility, (2) ingenuity, (3) fruition, (4) knowledge, to gain positive (5) comportment and (6) intercommunication skills with the understanding that (7) contentment and (8) greed can detour you from understanding your (9) senses and becoming a (10) Christian. Love! Live! Life!

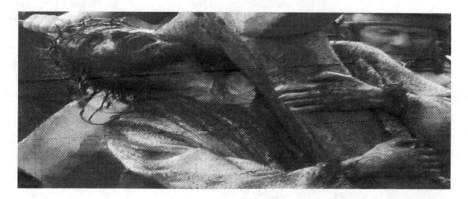

Empower Yourself

Become a Business Owner By Joining S. Seller and Joining our Network Corporation

Bronze S. Seller

1. If you sell 10 books. You will receive $100.00. If you refer the book to 10 people and they purchase the book. You will receive $110.00 person to purchase the book.

Silver S. Seller

1. If you sell 20 books. You will receive $200.00. If you refer the book to 20 people and they purchase the book. You will receive $210.00 person to purchase the book.

Gold S. Seller

1. If you sell 30 books. You will receive $300.00. If you refer the book to 30 people and they purchase the book. You will receive $310.00 person to purchase the book.

Platinum Seller

1. If you sell 40 books. You will receive $400.00. If you refer the book to 40 people and they purchase the book. You will receive $410.00 person to purchase the book.

Network Corporation

About Us

✓ Network Corp. Inc. oversees a community based, comprehensive network system across the United States.

✓ Network Corp collaborated with dozens of state and local agencies to accomplish its main goal, which is to improve citizens with networking possibilities and resources. Today, Network Corp. works to make networking easier for its consumers and provide financial, leadership, and decision making skills to meet community needs.

Mission Statement

✓ The mission of Network Corp., a for-profit business, is to maximize the effectiveness of networking by providing resources to citizens across the United States.

Vision Statement

 Network Corp strives to be the premier networking provider to residents across the United States.

Value Statements

We at Network Corp. hold these values to be fundamental:

 People: We respect each person as a member of the networking community. Involvement and teamwork determine our future.

Service Excellence: We are committed to our standards of service excellence and dedicated to exceeding the expectation of those we serve.

Responsibility: We accept personal accountability for the work we do

Communication: We promote open communication that fosters partnership and enhances timely, effective, and appropriate responses.

Innovation: We are committed to a supportive environment that encourages new ideas and creativity.

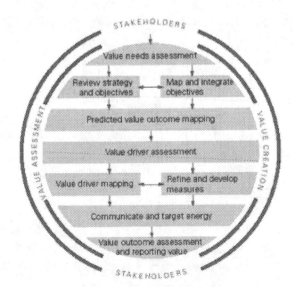

How to Join?

✓ To join Network Corporation, one must fill out an application and submit a fee for membership: $50.00

✓ What do you receive for the membership?

✓ Membership Card

✓ Network of over 500,000 people

✓ Free Copy of the book titled "The Tr-Youth." with present value of $42.00

✓ Each month you will be eligible for a Network Corp Bonus.

✓ Each month you will be eligible for a Network Corp Incentive Drawing.

Levels of Membership

Bronze Operational

- If you get 10 members to join Network Corp., you will receive $166.67
- If you get 20 members to join Network Corp., you will receive $250.00

Silver Tactical

- If you get 30 members to join Network Corp., you will receive $250.00

    - Personal Website
    - Business Cards
    - Dinner with CEO and/or Gift Certificate

Gold Strategic

- If you get 50 + members to join Network Corp.,

  - You will receive $1000.00

Platinum
- If you get 100 member to join Network Corp
- You do not pay annually dues for lifetime.
- You do not pay for any conferences and have a buddy pass for all lectures.
- You get Platinum Business Pin, Shirt, Jacket, and Hat
- You will receive a bonus check of $2000

Why Join?

Rich Relationships

- *Rich relationships lead to much more than money. They lead to success, fulfillment, and wealth.*
- *Free Lectures discussing some of the below pinpoints......*

  1. *Do you have a little black book?*
  2. *Take a moment and list your top ten most powerful connections (the people who can make things happen, and make things happen for you.*
  3. *Then ask yourself, "What have I done for these people lately?*
  4. *Who can you count on?*
  5. *Who is counting on you?*
  6. *Who would call you at three in the morning?*
  7. *Who would you call at three in the morning?*

Network Corporations pinpoints how ...

- To earn the respect of a powerful mentor without begging.

- To build stronger relationships with customers, vendors, friends, co-workers

- To connect with powerful people and how not to connect with powerful people

- To say the right things to the right people

- To maximize your connections so they benefit from you and more important, how you benefit from them

A Young Doctor with Young Experience equipped with OLD Thoughts

This book will help you navigate the interior landscape of your self, overcome barriers to your fulfillment, and discover a wholehearted and total vision for your life. Once you've uncovered your dreams, this book will provide you with the knowledge and tools to make those dreams you hold for your life real.

In Empowerment you will learn the specific actions you can take to create prosperity and quality of life, achieve success in your work, transform negative emotion, deepen your spirituality, and passion for life.

A sense of powerlessness and meaninglessness seems to lie at the root of most of the personal, family, and social disorders that plague us today. Empowerment and renewed meaning are essential ingredients in stress reduction, recovery, and healing.

NOTES

NOTES

NOTES

NOTES

NOTES

NOTES

NOTES

NOTES

NOTES

NOTES

NOTES

NOTES

NOTES

NOTES

NOTES

NOTES

NOTES

NOTES

NOTES

NOTES

NOTES

NOTES

NOTES

NOTES

NOTES

NOTES

NOTES

NOTES

NOTES

NOTES

NOTES